THE BOOK OF QUESTIONS:

BUSINESS, POLITICS and ETHICS

GREGORY STOCK, PH.D.

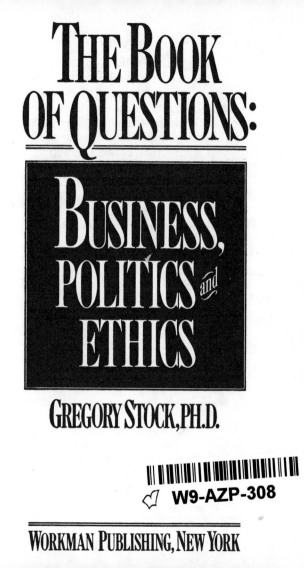

WORKMAN PUBLISHING, NEW YORK

Library of Congress
Cataloging-in-Publication Data
Stock, Gregory.
The Book of Questions: Business, Politics, and
Ethics.
1. Ethics—Miscellanea. 2. Business ethics—
Miscellanea. 3. Political ethics—Miscellanea. I.
Title. BJ1031.S76 1991   90-50953
172—dc20   CIP

ISBN 1-56305-034-X

Cover illustration: Tom Lulevitch
Cover design: Paul Hanson

Workman Publishing Company, Inc.
708 Broadway
New York, NY 10003

Manufactured in the United States of America
First printing
2 4 6 8 10 9 7 5 3 1

To Spike Carlson
for his courage in the face of adversity

To John Summer
for a conversation that once helped me
find my way

To Dick Haskell
for a random comment long ago
about Gandhi

and

To all those others
who are trying to make a difference

ACKNOWLEDGMENTS

Many, through their comments and encouragement, have helped improve this manuscript. In particular, I wish to thank Angelica Kusar, Don Ponturo, Marina Skumanich, Joseph Spieler, Katy Stock, Jane Stock, Gene Stock, Lois Swanson, and Fred Weber for their helpful review of a rough draft of the material; John Summer for his sundry suggestions for questions; Elisabeth Scharlatt for her editorial guidance; and David Breznau for his part in producing the original *Book of Questions*.

INTRODUCTION

Today our lives are intertwined to an extent unimaginable a century ago: Images from distant lands parade through our living rooms, population growth crams us together, goods and people shuttle between continents, environmental insults cast long shadows. Our lives touch not just family and friends, but countless others. Some of these people we encounter regularly; others we never meet but nonetheless affect through the choices we make. What we buy, how we live, what we say—each of our actions, like the proverbial pebble splashing into the pond, spreads ripples of effects into the the world.

The questions raised here—of justice, freedom, equity, leadership, generosity, responsibility—are joined by a common thread: They arise out of our interactions with others. Difficult choices develop whenever our individual designs collide with our larger responsibilities to our community, the people who work with us, the organizations to which we belong. The issues are timeless, but the forms they assume now are often without precedent. Our challenge is to live up to our values and standards of ethics in this increasingly complex world, and to align our behavior with our larger vision of society.

In this book of questions, I look primarily at two agents holding powerful sway over us: commerce and government. Commerce organizes human endeavor while government seeks to maintain a stable societal framework. But how deeply will we allow these agents to penetrate our lives? How shall we deal with them? It is so easy for most of us to live without considering whether our behavior is in harmony with our values that too often we see only in hindsight the implications of our actions. How else can one explain why some people with immense wealth will risk everything on what is, for them, petty fraud, or why others, hotly pursuing goals they *should* know are hollow, will neglect those they love most?

Today, there is much to be cynical about: crime without punishment, poverty abiding in the midst of riches, greed and corruption masquerading as public service. It is easy to complain. But can you and I offer solutions? One thing is certain: Even with the best of intentions, we will be pulled in many different directions. Satisfying solutions do not always exist. Supporting one worthy cause may deny others, and in such cases there must be losers and we must decide who they will be.

But this book is not a quiz on ethics or public policy. There are no right or wrong answers to the questions found here, only honest and dishonest ones. We each have our own answers, and as we reflect alone or in the company of others, we may find that our answers change. This is as it should be. With these questions, our answers are not as important as whether we reach them in a way that brings us to better understand both the issues and ourselves.

To struggle with dilemmas that touch us is a good way to clarify our values, and to listen is a crucial part of this process. When we consider new perspectives, it not only challenges our convictions, it also teaches us about other people. It is surprising how often someone we think we know will respond to a question about values in a way we would never have predicted.

In a culture so full of distractions as our own, how much time do we take to think and talk about our values? The questions in this book can help us take that time because they give us an easy way of broaching such topics. Allow yourself to be swept up by the situations here. Imagine that the choices you face here are real and that your decisions will have consequences.

When related ideas and questions come up, follow them wherever they lead. Regard these questions as your own and adjust the conditions they pose so as to make the choices more meaningful to you. But don't be too easy on yourself. Ethical dilemmas are of value precisely because they have no easy answers.

Finally, keep in mind that most of us are capable of far more than we ever dare attempt. We each can choose for ourselves the marks we will try to leave on the world, and we each *can* make a difference.

* Selected questions are marked with an asterisk to indicate that follow-up questions can be found at the back of the book.

THE BOOK OF QUESTIONS:

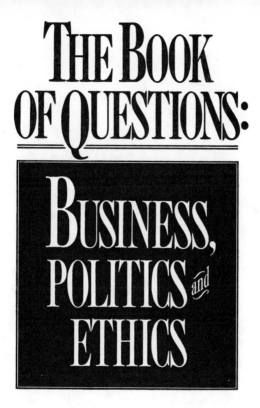

BUSINESS, POLITICS and ETHICS

1

If you were determining who could immigrate here, would you let in those you thought would contribute the most to our country or those most in need of refuge?

2

If you ran a hospital, what policy would you set for dealing with emergency patients who arrive without health insurance or money?

3

Would you vote for a mayoral candidate who was honest, competent, and concurred with your position on most issues if you knew she was also an alcoholic who was sexually promiscuous and three times divorced?

4

If you smoked marijuana as a teenager and now were filling out an employment questionnaire asking whether you had ever used drugs, how would you respond? Assume you must sign an affadavit swearing to the truth of your statements.

5

If you knew that when you died you would immediately be reincarnated as the next baby born in the world, how—if at all—would your attitudes change about foreign aid, international politics, and birth control? (Note that ninety percent of all births now are in the poorer regions of the world.)

6

If you discovered that your closest friend at work had for years forged records and stolen from the company, what would you do? What if you hardly knew the thief?

7

If because of intolerance you were going to miss a wonderful chance at a promotion, might you lie to hide your religious beliefs?

8

If there were government representatives whose sole job was to protect the interests of generations yet to be born, what government policies do you think they might try to change? Would you favor having such officials?*

9

If you went to a store and found it was being peacefully picketed by striking employees, would you be more likely to go elsewhere or to shop there anyway? Why?

10

If you knew you were destined to never achieve anything of real importance, how would it change your goals and attitudes?*

11

Imagine you lost your thumb because of your own carelessness with a power saw. If you knew you could collect a lot of money even though the accident had been your fault, would you sue the manufacturer? What if you knew that to win the suit you would have to lie under oath?*

12

If a policeman offered—for $50 in cash—not to write you an $80 speeding ticket, would you pay him? If so, what if you hadn't been speeding?

13

If the owner of a local gas station were caught dumping fifty gallons of used motor oil into a city storm drain, what would you like his punishment to be? What if your neighbor were caught doing the same with one gallon?

14

If a friendly teenager stopped you outside a liquor store and tried to give you money to buy him a six-pack of beer, what would you do? Why?

15

Should there be a limit to the personal wealth one individual is allowed to amass? If so, how much is "too much"?

16

If a drunken guest at a party of yours said good-bye and, keys in hand, headed for his car, would you try to stop him? If so, how far would you be willing to go to keep him from driving?

17

If you bought something and broke it the next day, but in such a way that you could easily claim it had been broken when you got it, would you return the item?

18

Imagine you were a finalist in a contest paying a million dollars to whoever did the most good in the coming year—as judged by a panel of certified philanthropists. If the rules allowed you to spend no more time and money than you could comfortably afford, what would you do?

19

Are you more interested in international, national, state, or local news? Which has more impact on your life?

20

If the only way to avoid disastrous global warming were to halve our current consumption of energy, would you do so voluntarily or only under duress?*

21

If our country could earn substantial revenue by contracting for a yearly fee to defend foreign countries against invasion, would you want it to do so? Assume the contracts would be drawn up to guarantee massive aerial bombardment of any country mounting an invasion across our clients' borders?*

22

What would you do if you found out that a recently hired co-worker was making a third more than you for the same job you were doing?

23

Were it technologically feasible, would you favor installing monitors on roads so that all speeding and parking violators were automatically ticketed? If not, is it because you feel the laws are unfair or because you feel they should not be rigidly enforced?*

24

If a ninety-year-old friend, bedridden and in chronic pain, said he had decided it was time to "check out" and asked you—as the only person left who might understand—to get him some pills to do the job, would you try to assist him?*

25

Would you favor tripling the salaries of all public officials if you knew it would reduce corruption and improve government?

26

If you knew that all racial and ethnic discrimination in the country would disappear in twenty-five years, would you be pleased by the rapidity of the change or upset by its slowness?

27

Would you rather have a legal system that *never* punishes the innocent but often lets the guilty go free, or a system that *sometimes* punishes the innocent but never frees the guilty?

28

If permanent world peace could be gained by obliterating one country, would you be willing to select the country to be sacrificed? If so, which would you choose and why?

29

If you had to fire a problem employee, would you be more inclined to give the minimum or maximum notice possible? Why?

30

Should there be laws to regulate the behavior of consenting adults? If so, what—if anything—do you feel should be the punishment for a prostitute and her client? for two friends who insist on betting with each other on football?

31

If a casual acquaintance asked you how much your salary was, would you reveal it? What about a friend? If not, why not?*

32

If you knew it would, within twenty years, halve the incidence of violent crime, would you want to eliminate all physical violence from television and film?

33

Assume you have been elected to the legislature and now must cast the deciding vote in determining whether or not abortions will be legally available to women in your state. If you knew that your deeply felt position on this issue were contrary to that held by the vast majority of the voters you represent, would you cast your vote according to your beliefs or theirs?*

34

If you had to choose between two paths for our country—one leading to military supremacy and a weak economy, the other to economic supremacy and a weak military—which would you pick?

35

Have your biggest professional successes resulted from following well-thought-out plans or from taking advantage of unanticipated opportunities?

36

If, while surgically removing a lump from your cheek, your doctor inadvertently cut a nerve and caused one side of your mouth to be paralyzed, would you sue? Imagine you have a good case, but the surgeon is without insurance and will have to personally pay any settlement.

37

If in order to take advantage of an investment opportunity you needed a partner you could trust, whom would you pick? Why?

38

You are ruler of the land and it is budget time. If your art council were adamantly supporting people whose work you thought offensive—music sounding like traffic and paintings resembling kindergarten scrawls—would you overrule them and cut these items or defer to their artistic judgment?*

39

If you were a high-school teacher, would you feel it was your job to teach moral and ethical values, or just scholastic skills?

40

Your business, which employs a hundred people, has only an even chance of making it through the year. If this gets out, your suppliers are likely to stop giving you credit and force you into bankruptcy; but if you don't tell your employees, they may be caught unprepared and suffer great hardship. Would you tell your employees the truth?

41

If everyone in your community would be paid $5,000 to allow a disposal site for toxic chemicals to be located nearby, would you support or oppose its construction? Assume the plant design was certified by the government as absolutely safe.*

42

For a yearly rental fee of one-third of your car's value, would you display billboard-like ads on its doors?

43

Should a sucker get an even break? If a stranger tried to make a big bet with you about something you were absolutely certain about, would you try to dissuade him or just take his money?

44

Ambushed by guerillas, your military unit suffers heavy casualties and several of your men are captured. To get vital information that would save the lives of those men, would you, if necessary, torture a captured enemy soldier?

45

The President of the United States earns about $250,000 a year while the president of Ford earns some $2,000,000. Do you believe these salaries are what they should be? If not, what salaries would you recommend?

Do you think people now behave less or more ethically than they did a decade ago? How has your own behavior changed during this period?*

If a person with whom you were negotiating a lucrative business arrangement lost his temper and started insulting you, would you be likely to pull out of the deal?

48

Do you feel that laws are more frequently too strict or too lenient?

49

If you could legally sell your vote in the next presidential election by giving someone a signed blank ballot, would you? If so, how much would you ask for it?

50

Do you believe that government services such as education, health care, and police protection should be equally good everywhere, or that wealthier communities should have better services because they pay more taxes?

51

To what organization do you feel the deepest sense of loyalty? What most ties you to this group?

52

A friend tells you of a soon-to-be-announced merger that his cousin, who worked on the deal, just told him about. If the story convinced you a fortune could be made on the company's stock, would you buy it? If so, would the fact that you were committing a crime by engaging in "insider" trading bother you?*

53

If an eccentric millionaire hired you to spend $10 million to help society, what would you do with the money?

54

If there were a subliminal advertising technique so effective it could induce people to make purchases they would otherwise resist, would you want to ban it? What about an equally effective technique that wasn't subliminal but was just a great pitch strongly appealing to people's hopes and fears?

55

If you had no health insurance and got an illness that would be fatal without an operation you couldn't afford, would you feel wronged if you were denied the procedure?

56

If late one night you left a door at work unlocked and someone vandalized the place, would you admit your carelessness? Assume no one knows you were there.

57

If you were a psychiatrist, and during therapy a patient revealed he had once murdered someone, would you violate your oath of confidentiality and tell the authorities? If not, what if he later told you he had been imagining killing his boss?

58

If the President called up and said he would do his best to implement any one program or policy you chose, what would you want done?

59

You fire an incompetent employee who then files a hefty discrimination suit against you. If the charges were a complete fabrication but you knew that a court battle would be expensive, time consuming, and of uncertain outcome, would you be willing to settle out of court for a few thousand dollars?

60

Could you feel "free" if you were prohibited by law from changing careers? What if you were allowed to but knew you could never afford to take such a risk?*

61

If you took a job in a country where bribery was an accepted business practice, would you refuse to arrange such payments and thereby risk losing business? If so, what would you do if you learned that a local employee of yours was still paying the customary bribes?

62

If you knew that millions of people would model their lives after you, would you change anything about the way you live? When have you changed your own behavior to try to influence someone else?

63

If a benign, genetically engineered virus were able to miraculously slow human aging, would you want it released? Assume that as soon as this occurred everyone's life expectancy would double.*

64

If your city were building a public transit system and wanted to raze your home to do so, would you try to block the project? If, for similar reasons, the government were forcing you to leave an apartment you had long rented, would you expect special compensation?

65

Would you rather live in a country where your religion was the state religion, or in one where church and state were separate and all religions were treated equally?

66

Would you like to see the United Nations establish a dozen television channels and allow all governments and political groups to broadcast whatever messages they wished to the world? Assume these channels, received by all TVs, would never be censored. How—if at all—might such free communication change our world?

67

Would you rather go to a very talented doctor who is unscrupulous or to a less talented one who is completely trustworthy? What about a lawyer or an auto mechanic?

68

What, if anything, is more important for a business than making a profit?*

69

If you left your company for a better position with a competitor, might you reveal to your new employers the confidential information contained in a valuable marketing plan of your old firm?*

70

If a brother or sister of yours were caught driving drunk and you had to set the punishment, what would it be? How would it differ if you knew your choice would become the standard punishment for every drunk driver?*

71

Terrorists take a planeload of tourists hostage and threaten to kill them unless a dozen imprisoned comrades are freed. If you knew that meeting the hijackers' demands would gain the hostages' release, while refusing would bring their death, what would you vote to do? Assume you are part of a panel appointed to decide the issue.

72

Presented with two applicants for a word processing job, would you hire the one who was friendly, attractive, and capable of doing an adequate job, or the one who was far more capable but had a sour disposition and was ugly?*

73

Would you rather your work were more or less of a team effort than it is now?

74

When you find you no longer need something that belongs to you, is your first impulse to sell it, give it away, store it, or throw it out? How much does your attitude depend on the item's monetary value?

75

Have you ever cheated an employer by secretly spending time on personal projects while pretending to be working? What if one day you caught an employee of yours doing this?

76

If you knew you could double your money in two years by investing in a company whose activities you strongly disapproved of, would you do it?

77

When you make a decision, are you generally more concerned about its immediate consequences or its long-range impact? How much have you changed in this regard over the past decade?

78

Do you think our penal system should be more concerned with removing criminals from society, detering crime, or rehabilitating wrongdoers?

79

After testing for radon, you discover your home is too hazardous to live in; furthermore, since your insurance doesn't cover such a thing, the house will become worthless as soon as the contamination is revealed. If you knew you could destroy the test results and sell the house without anyone ever knowing what had occurred, might you do so?

80

What would be your biggest misgiving about becoming a business partner with your brother or sister?

81

Would you like every product to be taxed so that its price includes payment for what it indirectly costs society? For example, should the price of cigarettes be raised so that smokers pay for the added medical costs they incur? Should gasoline taxes be increased to that motorists bear the costs of pollution and acid rain?

82

At what age—if any—should you yourself have to retire, even if you want to work and can still do your job well?*

83

Would you favor decriminalizing all drugs if you knew it would dramatically reduce violent crime but greatly increase the death toll from drug abuse?

84

What is the biggest effort you have ever made to influence public policy? If you decided you had to do something about the public issue you feel most strongly about, what could you do that would have the most impact?

85

Which of your friends—had they nowhere else to turn—would you help extricate from financial straits by loaning a large part of your savings? Would you draw up a written agreement for such a loan?

86

If you, as owner of a company, had to either abruptly lay off loyal employees or suffer losses heavy enough to imperil the company, which would you do?

87

Do you believe that wealth in our society is fairly apportioned according to what people contribute? If not, what is the most glaring inequity you know?

88

If you got people to buy shares in a new business you were starting and the business failed despite your best efforts, would you feel you should pay back the money they invested?

89

If no foreign military threat existed, what beyond maintaining society's legal and economic framework would you want our government to do?*

90

If you could get away with it, would you apply for life insurance without revealing a fatal pre-existing illness such as AIDS?

91

How would it affect your opinion of your best friend if you discovered that he or she had made an airline reservation for the heavily overbooked Christmas holidays not in order to fly somewhere, but in order to get a free ticket by volunteering to be bumped from the flight?

92

If you had two choices—paying for a poor, unwed teenager's abortion, or paying fifty times more to support and educate her child—which would you do? What if, as a nation, we faced that same choice for one million babies a year?

93

For how long should you (or your heirs) be allowed to receive fees and royalties from something you invent?*

94

If people in underdeveloped countries were starving because of crop failures and we had no extra grain to send them, would you favor letting them starve or giving them the grain eaten by the livestock we raise? (Note that some eighteen pounds of grain are consumed for every pound of beef produced.)

95

When you vote, are you swayed more by a candidate's position on issues or by a candidate's character and personality? Do you feel you get a true impression of either during an election campaign?

96

If someone working for you made a costly mistake and you realized that your instructions should have been clearer, would you be more likely to describe the incident to your superior in a way that protected your subordinate or yourself?

97

Would you rather live in a democracy run by inept, corrupt leaders or in a dictatorship run by capable, honest ones?

98

When is the last time you did something solely to help the larger community beyond your family and friends?

99

In your view, can a government be moral even while doing what would be considered immoral for an individual—murder, theft, and lying, for example.

100

If you own a large piece of land, should you and your descendants be allowed to "own" it forever or should the land someday become public property?*

101

If a foreign nation refused to stop dumping dangerous wastes into the ocean, what—all else failing—would be the most drastic step you would favor taking to stop them?*

102

If your spouse were killed in an airplane crash involving no negligence, how much compensation—if any—would you feel you deserved? What if he or she were struck by lightning?*

103

Would you rather become extremely successful as the result of a lucky break, a smart gamble, or hard work?

104

If your sister were on life-support and in a coma following a car crash, and you were told that if she lived she would almost certainly be both physically and mentally handicapped, would you want to keep her alive or let her die? Would this be better for her or easier for you?

105

If you and a close friend were partners in a very lucrative business and had such a serious disagreement that you decided to dissolve the partnership, would you likely be more concerned about remaining friends or making a good deal?

106

If you were single and began to feel strongly attracted to someone you saw regularly at work, would you be inclined to avoid or seek romantic involvement?*

107

Which of the following programs would you fund if you had to choose only one of them: a massive public health program that would increase life expectancy by two years; an overhaul of our educational system that would make our primary schools the best in the world; a housing program that would give everyone an adequate place to live?

108

Do you think you would be more or less easily corrupted by power than your closest friend?

109

Imagine that one day your widowed father, who was very wealthy and very old, told you he was going to change his will and give all his money to charity. Assuming you knew he would not change his mind and was quite sane, would you consider trying to block your disinheritance by having him declared incompetent?

110

Do you think you are knowledgeable enough to make wise choices among alternative approaches to complex issues such as improving education, combatting drug addiction, improving health care, controlling pollution, and strengthening the economy?*

111

Whom would you punish more harshly: someone who knowingly dumped chemicals likely to cause a number of cancer deaths, or someone who fatally shot a person in a brawl?*

112

If you were selling a car and knew about a subtle but serious problem, would you tell prospective buyers?

113

Do you pay too much in taxes? If so, what do you feel would be a fair amount for you to pay? Would you voluntarily pay twice the taxes you do now if it would confer your standard of living on all who are poorer than you?*

114

How much additional income would you need to meaningfully change your day-to-day life?*

115

While traveling in India, you see something you want to buy and are quoted a price far below what it would cost back home. If the amount meant little to you, would you nonetheless try to bargain for a still lower price? If so, why?

116

If your sixteen-year-old daughter vandalized someone's property, would you feel financially liable? If so, how old would she have to be before you no longer felt you needed to pay for her mistakes?*

117

If you knew that the innate abilities of different ethnic groups were unequal, how—if at all—would it change your attitudes about discrimination? What if you knew that all groups were essentially the same?*

118

If, to escape financial ruin, your company were reorganized and you were let go, what severance pay would you feel entitled to?

119

If you were running for governor of your state, what details of your life would you refuse to discuss with a journalist questioning you?*

120

Do you generally round off monetary amounts in your favor or in other people's?

121

If you had to make a difficult sacrifice in either your career or your marriage, which would you choose? For example, what if you had to either forgo a long-sought promotion or move overseas for two years, uprooting your whole family against their wishes?

122

In what ways are your ethics in business different from those in your personal life? Do you think you have a better reputation in your professional or personal dealings?

123

If your government killed many people by wrongly bombing another country, would you feel a personal responsibility to try to make amends?

124

You go to lunch with a group of people from work and they all order expensive meals and drinks while you, having had a late breakfast, order almost nothing. Would you protest if someone proposed dividing the bill equally?*

125

Do you behave as a "good citizen," even when you know your small action will make no real difference—for example, do you ever pick up other people's litter?

126

In exchange for great wealth and power, would you give up your privacy and live always in the public eye?

Six months after being hired, you become ill and are temporarily bedridden. How long do you think your employer should wait before permanently replacing you? What if you had been working there for ten years?*

Would you rather your boss were better at his job or nicer as a person?

129

If it were up to you, would it be mandatory for households to separate and recycle aluminum, glass, and newspaper?

130

Would you be more likely to cheat your company if your personal finances were in good shape but you hated your boss, or if you liked your boss but were in dire financial straits?

131

Which of your friends do you think would like you more if you were more successful? How do you imagine these friends would treat you differently if you lost your job and most of your money?

132

If after you completed a call at a pay phone, a recorded voice said you owed two more dollars, would you pay it? Assume you know that nothing would happen if you just walked away.*

133

Given a specific amount of money to use in fighting lung cancer, would you rather spend it on public education about smoking or on medical treatment for cancer patients?

134

If your business were going bankrupt and most of the company's debts would never be paid, would you use the company's few remaining assets to reimburse customers for unfilled orders, to pay employees their back wages, or to pay suppliers for the goods they had given you on credit? Assume you can do only one.

135

When you are shopping and drop a piece of fruit on the floor, do you put it back and take a new one or take the one you damaged?*

136

If you had health insurance that would cover any medical treatment, would you seek additional care for anything?*

137

If you knew that everyone in the industrialized world would match your contribution to a massive program to improve conditions in underdeveloped lands, what fraction of your assets and future income would you pledge irrevocably to such a cause?

138

For a sizable payment, would you go on TV and enthusiastically endorse a product you thought mediocre?

139

If you and your family emigrated to Spain, how long would it be before you spoke Spanish in your home? Do you think you would lose your cultural identity if you had to give up your native tongue?*

140

Damning circumstantial evidence makes it very likely you will be convicted of a crime you did not commit. If you were offered a suspended sentence for pleading guilty, would you make the deal or fight the charges knowing full well you would probably end up spending a year in prison for the effort?*

141

If a brilliant tax expert could legally cut your taxes by ninety percent—but only by completely violating the spirit of the tax code—would you let him do it?

142

If after just completing an expensive training program provided by your employer you were offered a better position by another firm, would you feel all right about taking it?

143

Have you ever given a "gift" in the hope of gaining someone's help on a project of yours? What—if any—is the distinction between such gift giving and bribery?

144

If there were a military coup here and a powerful dictatorship took firm control of the government, would you be more inclined to try to influence its policies or to refuse any association with it?*

145

If you were President, under what circumstances—if any—would you lie to the country to gain public support?*

146

It is said that everyone has his price. If you were responsible for awarding a huge building contract and a construction firm wanted to influence your decision, what would be *your* price? Assume you were convinced you'd never be discovered.

147

Do you expect people who are working under your direction to work harder or put in longer hours than you yourself do?

148

Would you participate in a legal chain letter in which you would make $10,000 and ten strangers would lose $1,000 each? If not, why not?

149

When confronted with an ethical dilemma, do you chart a course based more on your own judgment or on the advice of others?

150

If you were in charge of filling a very desirable job at a medium-size company, how much of an edge would a friend or relative who wanted the position have over other applicants?

151

If the police caught your teenage daughter smoking marijuana from a plant she had grown in the woods, what would you want them to do? What if instead she were caught using psychedelic mushrooms she had found or cocaine she had bought?*

152

If you were running for public office and knew you could win the election by spreading malicious rumors about your opponent, would you smear him or her?

153

Civil wars, blood feuds, and religious struggles are notoriously difficult to end. Were you mired in such a conflict, could you ever agree to an amnesty that left unpunished those who had murdered your friends and family?

154

If you would get the same pay for any job, would you change your profession?

155

If one day at work you had an idea so good you knew you could either tell your boss about it and get a promotion or leave and set up a profitable company of your own, which would you be more inclined to do? Would your final choice hinge more on thoughts about the challenge of founding a company or the loyalty you owed your employer?

156

When is the last time you borrowed something from someone and didn't return it? At the time, how did you justify your actions to yourself?

Imagine your young daughter were struck and killed in front of your house by a speeding car driven by a drunk. If the driver were acquitted on some technicality and further legal action were hopeless, would you seek revenge?

158

If the decision were yours, would you permit general use of a potent flu vaccine that conferred lifetime immunity against the virus but caused a fatal reaction in one of every few hundred people who took it?

159

When doing business with strangers, do you generally approach a deal with more suspicion or trust? Do you begin a new romance any differently?

160

If you buy something at a price that pleases you and later discover you could have gotten it for less, how much does it disturb you?

161

Would you like to make it a crime to witness a serious felony such as murder and not report it to the police?*

162

If a powerful corporation thwarted all your legal efforts to stop them from dumping toxic chemicals into a stream near your home, would you be more likely to sell your home, try to live with the situation, or do something else?

163

If restoring this country's economic competitiveness meant tightening your belt and saving twenty percent of your earnings during the coming decade, would you be willing to do so?

164

Your boss, whom you neither like nor respect, is planning to retire soon from a job you badly want. If you knew that by fawning and currying favor you could probably get the position, would you do it?

165

If you were a salesperson working on commission, might you sometimes misrepresent a product to sell it?

166

If you could specify the philosophy the government used in raising money, would you choose an approach that falls more heavily on the wealthy (graduated income and property taxes) or equally on all (uniform sales taxes and usage fees)?*

167

If you had to choose between a satisfying job with little security and a secure job with little satisfaction, which would you take? Has your attitude about this changed over time?

168

Generally, do you work harder to earn praise and reward or to avoid criticism and punishment? All told, have you yourself dispensed more criticism or praise?

169

Do you consider it more important for government to foster a society with prosperity, freedom, or security for its citizens?

170

If you knew that famine and disease brought about by overpopulation would claim a quarter of the babies born in this decade, how much of the defense budget would you divert to programs to reduce the birth rate? Assume there is *no* other source of money.

171

If your daughter injured your grandchild by taking drugs during her pregnancy, would you want her criminally punished in any way? What if she neglected the child after birth?*

172

If the President addressed the nation and asked us each to find one thing we could do to improve our country, what—if anything—would you do? Would you be more likely to do something if the President went on to say that he personally would pick up trash along the highways for several hours a week to show that no one was too important to do something?

173

If you hoped to move elsewhere soon, but knew that to win a long-sought promotion you would have to claim that you planned to stay in town for many years, what would you say?

174

Would you rather have a leader who was more concerned with making this country prosperous over the next five years, or with ensuring our prosperity several decades from now?

175

If you were financially ruined by someone who cleverly deceived and cheated you, would you be more interested in getting revenge or in putting your life back together?

176

Would you be willing to write a good character reference for an old friend you liked a lot but knew was undependable and a bit of a scoundrel?

177

Do you think it should be against the law for someone to urinate on a copy of the United States Constitution? If so, what do you think the punishment for repeated offenses should be?*

178

What financial transaction of yours would be most difficult to justify to others if it became public knowledge?*

179

If everyone would follow your lead, would you adjust your life so as to sharply reduce the mileage you drive? If the price of gasoline doubled, would you use your car much less than you do now?

180

Where you work, money is being collected for a lavish retirement party for someone you strongly dislike; you, of course, are expected to contribute your share. How large a contribution request would it take to make you protest or refuse?

181

If you could stop all cigarette smoking by releasing a virus that would destroy every tobacco plant in the world, would you?

182

How much of your income would you be willing to pay in taxes to make it possible to walk anywhere, anytime, without fear of violent crime? If you knew that all such crime could be eliminated by having everyone's location constantly monitored electronically, would you be in favor of it?

183

Does it offend you when you are misled with half-truths in a business deal? What do you see as the ethical distinction between lying and intentionally leading people astray by cleverly omitting key parts of a story?

In some hospitals it is common for physicians to use gifts and favors to buy patient referrals from the emergency-room staff. If you became director of such a hospital, would you ignore the practice or try to stop it?

185

If you were President, would you be willing to help create a powerful global government that could settle all international disputes? Assume you would have to agree to submit to all its decisions.

186

Do you ever make expensive personal phone calls on a company phone? If so, how do you justify this to yourself?

187

Would you rather be a respected judge, an acclaimed actor, a renowned athlete, or an admired scientist? What most appeals to you about the position you chose?

188

If someone you had just hired wasn't doing a very good job, would you be more inclined to get rid of him or try to help him improve his performance?

189

Sometimes the boundary between right and wrong is the same as that between legal and illegal, but not always: Do you more frequently do lawful things you feel are wrong, or unlawful things you feel are all right?*

190

If it were possible to double expenditures on education and child care by denying all heroic medical procedures to anyone judged to be within a year of death, would you want to do so?*

191

If a wealthy uncle died and left everything to you, would you fight other relatives who threatened to contest the will unless you shared the estate with them? Assume you think they have no reasonable claim but may create a bitter enough legal battle to use up most of the inheritance.

192

Do you think that the right of a woman to have children should ever be restricted? If so, under what circumstances?*

193

If it could be guaranteed that someone guilty of armed robbery would not commit another crime, would you favor a punishment involving no prison term? If so, what might you suggest?

194

If a company invented and patented something that would greatly benefit society—for example, a device that dramatically reduced automobile emissions—and then decided to market it at an outlandish price, would you want the government to intervene in the public's interest?

195

What would you do if you shook hands on what seemed an excellent price for something valuable you were selling, and then someone else offered you twice as much? Assume you could—if you chose—break the first deal with impunity.

196

If you discovered that someone working for you had blackmailed a supplier in order to get delivery of materials you vitally needed, what would you do?*

197

If you were cheated by a business but didn't have the resources to pursue a court battle, what would you do?

198

If you discovered that the hospital you worked in was staying afloat by charging the government for unnecessary medical procedures, would you blow the whistle, try to stop the practice, or do nothing?*

199

If a waitress intentionally neglected to charge you for part of your meal, would you say anything about it? Would you tip her extra?*

200

If you bought a lawnmower with a one-year, no-questions-asked guarantee of satisfaction and happily used it for ten months before deciding to move to a high rise, would you ask for a refund?

201

If you were a policeman in a crime-ridden area and a cafe owner promised you a free meal anytime you cared to stop by, would you take him up on the offer? Assume you believe his primary aim is to expand the police presence at his restaurant.

202

Whom at work do you trust enough to tell a secret that, if revealed, would cost you your job?

203

If someone working for you came up with a great idea, would you be more likely to overstate or understate your contribution when describing it to others?

204

Would you rather work with people who are less or more talented than you?

205

If all public officials found guilty of accepting bribes were to suffer the same punishment and you could set that punishment, what would it be?

206

What do you feel society owes you simply because you are a citizen and a human being? What do you feel you owe in return?

207

If cost and quality would be equivalent, would you rather repair or replace something when it breaks? Which do you think would be better for our economy?

208

Do you make important professional decisions any more decisively now than you did five years ago? When you reverse a decision, is it usually because you become aware of important new information or because you have a change of heart?*

209

To get rid of a problem employee, might you recommend him to someone else without mentioning his obvious flaws?

210

Have you ever taken a sick day from work when you weren't sick? If so, the last time you did it how did you justify your action to yourself?

211

What would you do if you found out that you had been working unknowingly with dangerous carcinogens for several years while your company's management had hidden the dangers from you?

212

When you spend money, do you consider who is profiting from your purchases?

213

If you had to decide whether or not the government would spend one million dollars on a highway safety feature you knew would save one life, would you spend the money? What is the maximum you would be willing to spend to save that life? What about to educate and care for an abandoned child?*

214

If you knew that someone selling property you wanted was so desperate he would take whatever you offered, what portion of the property's value would you give him?

215

If you had a great job at a wonderful company, and then accidentally discovered that for years management had been doctoring the books to steal money from the absentee owner, what would you do? How much would your actions be influenced by whether you liked the managers?

216

If you knew that violent crime could be reduced by eighty percent by outlawing the private possession of firearms for any purpose whatsoever—including hunting—would you favor such a law?

217

Would you prefer a President who had previously been a skillful and savvy politician, a brilliant science administrator, a writer of unbending moral integrity, or a highly respected military officer? Why?

218

If it were proposed that many important public policy decisions would henceforth be made not by elected officials but by representative "juries" of citizens chosen by lot, would you support the change? Would you be more confident in the integrity of random citizens or elected officials?*

219

Can you imagine any professional or financial setback so ruinous it would bring you close to suicide?*

220

What rights are so important that if the government tried to take them—not from you, but from others—you would be prepared to run great risks to fight what was happening? For what rights would you risk death to keep for yourself?

221

If what you earned were to fairly reflect what you contribute, how much would you be paid? Do you think others would agree with you? Where you work, who—if anyone—makes a lot more or less than they deserve?

222

When many years from now you look back on your life, do you think you will be more disturbed by the times you tried and failed, or by the times you found excuses and didn't try?

223

Many of the architectural treasures we so value—the Taj Mahal, Versailles, the Pyramids—were created using money or labor extracted from an unwilling populace. If you could go back and change these historical periods into ones that left no great legacies but had better standards of living for their people, would you?*

FURTHER
QUESTIONS

J ust as our responses to these questions are highly personal, so are our interpretations of them. One person may feel that a question deals with corruption in government; another may feel the same question deals with patriotism and honor; a third, that it is about money.

The purpose of these further questions is not to tell you what the important issues are in this book—that is up to you. These questions are here to extend some ideas posed in the earlier questions and to invite you to do likewise with the questions you find most intriguing.

Most of the value of questions comes from actively exploring them. Good questions generally lead not to definitive answers, but to more questions.

8

Does our current system of government adequately represent the interests of future generations? What responsibility do we have to conserve resources for those generations? to avoid environmental damage unlikely to be felt for a century? to keep world population at a sustainable level?

10

If you knew you would never move beyond your current level of professional success, how would it alter your life? What if you knew your real income would remain just what it is now? What if you knew that although your income would steadily increase, at retirement you would still have the same job you do now?

11

To what extent are others responsible for taking care of you when you suffer calamity? Obviously, the better the care provided to relieve such suffering the more it costs; what percentage of your income would you be willing to spend to provide a safety net for everyone? In your opinion, what care should such a safety net include—regardless of cost?

20

Would your enjoyment of life be significantly diminished if you could only own one small car or not use air-conditioning? If you were forced to sharply cut your material consumption, what would be the least painful way for you to do so?

21

If you were a citizen of a small country surrounded by powerful neighbors, would you favor purchasing such protection rather than trying to build an army of your own? Do you think contracts (always purely defensive) with the superpowers would stabilize or destabilize the world? If you were a citizen of a moderately powerful country and could save a lot of money by using such a contract, would you favor buying one contract and drastically cutting military spending?

23

If it were possible to do so, would you make the detection and punishment of *all* infringements of the law absolutely certain and automatic?

24

What if your terminally ill mother begged you to get sleeping pills for her so she could die with dignity? Would it matter if you were her only heir and might be prosecuted for doing so? Should physicians—under at least some circumstances—be allowed to assist in the death of patients who wish to die?

31

Why are most people in our culture so private about their finances? How would your life change if everyone knew all the details of yours? Do your friends know more about your finances or your love life?

33

To what extent do you feel that elected officials should try to reflect the attitudes of their constituents and to what extent should they disregard those attitudes and try to project their own personal visions of policy? For what offices must politicians have strong beliefs about policy in order to serve their constituents well? For what offices would it be better for them to change as prevailing opinion does?

38

If it were up to you, would you increase or decrease government support of the arts? Why?

41

Should nearby residents be paid to have such things as prisons, dumps, and other undesirable constructions located near them? If the government would pay communities for permits to locate such constructions nearby, do you think many communities would compete to have them? (Assume the government would get competitive bids and buy the cheapest permits offered.)

46

Many people feel the world is getting less ethical but few feel they themselves are becoming so. Do you think the explanation for this paradox is that people fail to see the truth about themselves or about others?

52

If you were caught trading on such inside information, what would be a just punishment? How would you punish a company treasurer who did not profit personally, but who helped a friend make a bundle in this way?

60

What does "freedom" mean to you? Is it important to you to have freedoms you are unable to exercise? What freedoms do you value most: the freedom to choose your occupation? to marry whomever you wish? to live where you want? to speak freely? to travel anywhere?

63

Do you think dramatically increasing human life expectancy would leave the world better or worse off a century from now? If death rates fell sharply, how do you think population growth could be checked? The current population explosion in the underdeveloped world stems from the imbalance between a gradually declining birth rate and a mortality rate *abruptly* lowered by advances in health and sanitation. Given this, if you could go back in time and slow these "advances," would you? If the only two ways of halting population growth without massive famine were to limit families to one child or to offer payments to anyone who would voluntarily end his life, which would you favor?

68

Should corporations try to behave as "moral" creatures, or is any sacrifice of profit a betrayal of the interests of the shareholders? Many parties are affected by any corporation: shareholders, employees, customers, suppliers, the surrounding community. Whose interests should be of primary concern to upper management? How strongly should the interests of others be considered? Should we judge corporations, just as we do people, on the basis of not only their success but also their integrity?

69

If you hired a new employee and he refused to tell you some important confidential information about his previous employer, would you value him more or less? How long do your commitments and loyalties persist after a professional relationship ends? When there is conflict between your new and old loyalties, which generally takes precedence?

70

If you had the power to mandate the installation in all cars of an alcohol-monitoring device that prevented anyone who had recently drunk alcohol from starting the car, would you do so? Would you similarly make it mandatory to wear seat belts?

72

In hiring someone, what criteria other than performance-related ones do you feel might rightly be considered? Would your feelings about a person's appearance, politics, ethnic background, or lifestyle influence you much in hiring or promoting someone? If not, might you still be somewhat influenced by other people's attitudes about such things?

82

If retirement were not automatic and mandatory and you had to determine whether a successful and powerful manager should retire, how would you do so? What about a somewhat eccentric seventy-five-year-old college professor working on her own research? If older people remained working for as long as they could, would this keep younger people out of positions of power too long or would it simply make better use of the talent and experience of the aged?

89

To what extent should government attempt to influence how wealth is distributed within a country? manage the economy? promote such activities as art, music, literature, sports, education? guarantee some basic level of health care and economic well-being for its citizens?

93

When a technological development arises inde-penently several times, the advance is probably a natural outgrowth of what has gone before; if so, why should society greatly reward the people who happen to be first to claim it? If patents and copyrights lasted only half as long as they do now, do you think innovation would be signifi-cantly reduced? What about prices? Should there be any limit to the profits someone can extract from an invention, a book, or a song? Royalties are still paid whenever the familiar four-line ditty starting "Happy Birthday to You" is sung in a film or play: Do you think there is a point at which such creations become so embedded in our culture that they should belong to everyone?

100

With so many billions of people and so few landowners, do you think the right of individuals to own and control land will one day have to change? Should primitive tribes be given permanent title to the land they are living on? Should property titles held by the heirs of long-dead nobles and aristocrats be honored? To what extent should people be able to do as they wish with land they "own," and to what extent should their treatment of the land be regulated by the present and future needs of society as a whole?

101

How can the international community force countries—both weak and strong ones—to follow accords that govern such global interests as pollution? For example, if most major nations became convinced that carbon dioxide emissions were resulting in highly destructive global warming, how could recalcitrant countries be forced to burn less fossil fuels?

102

Should victims of dramatic accidents receive any greater assistance than victims of more routine mishaps? Human error is bound to occur in certain activities: Should victims of such error be entitled to more help than victims of disease or other misfortunes where there are no culprits to blame?

106

Do you think it is important to avoid mixing business and romance? If you and an employee of yours became lovers, do you think you would be able to keep your professional and personal interactions separate? Would you even try? In what ways would you find it difficult to work for the person you now love?

110

Can democracy work in a country where most citizens are not knowledgeable enough to understand the complex issues confronting society? What about in a country where only a small fraction of the people participate in elections?

111

Is a crime any less serious if its impact is delayed rather than immediate? if its victims are faceless strangers rather than specific individuals? if its impact is indirect rather than direct? Is robbing a store by breaking and entering any worse than doing so by embezzlement?

113

Do you resent having to pay taxes? If so, why? What responsibilities do you feel toward other people in our society? What—if anything—do you do to increase the general good rather than that of yourself and your family? Our society offers us some measure of personal safety, political freedom, economic opportunity, health care, education, transportation, and other benefits; what do you feel are the two most important services our *government* provides you personally? Would you be willing to give them up if it meant you would pay no taxes?

114

If your income doubled, how long do you think it would take you to alter your spending habits so that you would have as many financial concerns as you do now?

116

What crimes—if any—might a child commit that a parent should be held criminally responsible for? Is there some level of supervision or control that a parent should by law have to maintain over a child? Who in our society should be most responsible for teaching values to the young?

117

Do you feel it is more important to give ethnic groups equal opportunity in different fields or to ensure that they achieve equal levels of success in those fields? Under what circumstances if any do you believe that government should regulate the ethnic diversity of a particular profession? How, if at all, would you compensate individuals for past discrimination against them or their ancestors?

119

How much do we have the right to know about the private lives of elected officials? If you decided to run for public office, what in your past would probably be most damaging to your campaign if the press got hold of the story? Might you lie about this if questions about it came up?

124

Over the long run, when you dine out with others do you pay more than the cost of what you consume, or less? How does your behavior in this regard compare with your generosity in other parts of your life?

127

Would your attitude about the length of time be different if you were the owner of the firm rather than the employee? If a critical job could not be done well by temporary help and yet you wanted to keep a position open for a woman who was going to be absent for a year because of pregnancy complications, what would you do? At what point must an employee—regardless of the nature of his personal problems—be fired if he cannot do his job?

132

In what ways—if any—do you apply looser ethical standards when you deal with large companies rather than individuals? For example, would you consider it theft to take a few tablets of paper home from an office at a big corporation? What about from a friend's house? If you do apply looser standards, does this mean that the increasing presence in your life of large corporations has made your overall behavior less ethical?

135

If you accidentally damaged merchandise in a store, would you tell someone or try to hide what you had done? What if the damage were so subtle you knew it would go unnoticed until someone bought the item and tried to use it? Would you ever buy something, use it, and return it just because you grew tired of it?

136

Do you think that—without severely restricting the treatments covered—we, as a society, will ever have the resources to make health care available to everyone? Do you believe that modern medicine will one day keep us healthy until near the time of death, or that it will never do more than postpone the time when chronic infirmity overtakes us? Will modern medicine eventually lead to lower overall health care costs in an individual's life, or will lifetime health costs rise as the frontiers of medical care are gradually rolled back?

139

When—if ever—should a minority group be forced to learn the language of the country in which it lives? Under what circumstances should a government make such things as ballots and government forms available in more than one language? When should government restrict the public use of a minority language?

140

Do you think it is rare for an innocent person to plead guilty to criminal charges? What would you guess is the percentage of convictions of people innocent of the charges against them? What about the percentage of acquittals of people guilty as charged?

144

If you knew you could bring about more good by collaborating with a detestable government rather than opposing it, which would you do? Do you think it would be possible for you to collaborate and yet remain untainted by the association?

145

Do you think a government official is justified in breaking the law under certain circumstances? If so, what laws—if any—do you think should be absolutely inviolate regardless of the circumstances?

151

Actions such as attempting suicide, using drugs, or even smoking cigarettes generally have far greater consequences for the person who does them than for others. To what extent should such matters be left to individual choice and to what extent should they be regulated by law? If there are to be laws to protect us from ourselves, how severely should violations be punished? For example, what would you do to someone who stubbornly insisted on swimming where it was forbidden because of dangerous currents?

161

How much responsibility do we as citizens have to participate in legal procedings that do not affect us directly? Would you try to avoid jury duty? What would you do if you witnessed an auto accident and knew that if you gave your name you would have to spend several days in court? If you witnessed a violent crime and were afraid you might be in danger if you became a witness, would you nonetheless call the police and tell them what you had seen?

166

Would you like our government to pay for its programs by raising money primarily from those who will benefit from those programs? If so, how should the many situations be handled where those who will benefit can't afford to pay—for example, care for the aged or poor?

171

How can parents who harm their children be punished in a way that doesn't bring further harm to the children one is trying to protect?

177

Should freedom of speech be limited to what we say, or should it include various actions we might take? Should actions that are offensive to many people and yet cause no one any injury be prohibited by the government? If not, is there any limit to how disgusting and offensive such actions could become before they were no longer tolerated? If so, what do you feel is the reason for prohibiting such acts, and how would you decide whether or not something should be prohibited?

178

Have you ever harshly criticized a public figure for conduct differing little from what you yourself have done at one time? If so, is it because your attitude about such conduct has changed, because you hold others to a higher standard than you hold yourself, or something else?

189

Are there any specific laws you regularly break? If so, would you be disappointed or pleased to learn that the person you most admire breaks these same laws? Do you think it causes problems to have laws that are routinely ignored? Are there any laws you feel should be kept on the books but not enforced?

190

Today, an ever larger fraction of health care is consumed during the last few years of life and thus is spent on the old and chronically ill. Do you feel that buying a few additional years of life for the elderly and infirm is a good way for our society to expend its resources? (Note that health care expenditures are now more than eleven percent of the GNP in the United States.)

192

If it became necessary to limit population growth, would you favor uniformly limiting everyone's right to have children, or basing this right on criteria such as the ability to care for them?

196

When a manager fosters an environment that is indifferent to questionable methods of achieving goals, to what extent should he be held accountable for resultant excesses, even if he is unaware of them?

198

Would it matter if you knew that your revelation would close the hospital and put you out of a job? What—if anything—do you think is the ethical distinction between fraudulently taking money from the government and fraudulently evading taxes so as not to give it to them?

199

What is the ethical difference between giving an extra tip to an employee who undercharges you, and impulsively reaching an understanding with that same employee to steal a small sum from the cash register and split the take?

208

Are you better at making decisions about professional or personal matters? In what ways do you handle dilemmas in these two realms differently? In which, for example, are you more inclined to be arbitrary or to make your decisions without seeking advice?

213

By evaluating the relative benefits of alternative uses for money, in essence policy makers do place a value on life. For example, it is estimated that giving routine tests for cervical cancer costs about $25,000 per life saved, installing air bags in cars costs some $300,000 per life saved, and meeting EPA standards for radium in drinking water would cost more than $2,000,000 per life saved (R. Cohen, *Journal of Health Physics*, 1980, vol. 38, 33). Given your attitude about the value of life and your understanding of our country's many financial needs, what price per life saved would you set as a cost threshold above which safety measures would be rejected?

218

How good do you think your decisions about complex issues would be if you were presented all relevant points of view and could ask questions of expert witnesses? Do you think that a panel of average citizens would make better or worse decisions than a group of elected politicians? Would you view the process of making decisions through randomly selected panels as democratic, or would you feel disenfranchised? Do you feel your vote is important? With voter turnout so low, does our government really reflect the will of its people? Is it important that it do so?

219

Do you think it is more difficult to handle a professional disaster, the loss of a loved one, or the loss of one's health? Which would you guess causes the most suicides? Would you rather be in a business debacle that left you bankrupt or in a car accident in which you suffered enough whiplash to give you chronic back pain? Can you imagine circumstances that might lead you to prefer the other?

223

What legacies would you like our society to leave to distant future generations? What sacrifices would you be willing to make to help this happen?

GREGORY STOCK IS the author of three other books: THE BOOK OF QUESTIONS, which has been translated into sixteen languages, THE KIDS' BOOK OF QUESTIONS, which is used in schools around the country, and LOVE AND SEX: THE BOOK OF QUESTIONS, which explores relationship issues. He received a doctorate in biophysics from the Johns Hopkins University in 1977, and has published numerous papers in biophysics and developmental biology. A Baker scholar, he received an MBA from the Harvard Business School in 1987. Now a visiting scholar at the University of California at Los Angeles, he is developing ideas for enhancing the effectiveness of private foundations and is completing a book on the implications of viewing human society as a superorganism.